YOUR KNOWLEDGE HAS VALUE

Anusua Chowdhury

Commercialization of the textile industry under British Rule

GRIN Verlag

Bibliografische Information der Deutschen Nationalbibliothek:

Die Deutsche Bibliothek verzeichnet diese Publikation in der Deutschen National-
bibliografie; detaillierte bibliografische Daten sind im Internet über http://dnb.d-
nb.de/ abrufbar.

Imprint:

Copyright © 2013 GRIN Verlag GmbH
Druck und Bindung: Books on Demand GmbH, Norderstedt Germany
ISBN: 978-3-656-55365-6

This book at GRIN:

http://www.grin.com/en/e-book/265739/commercialization-of-the-textile-industry-
under-british-rule

GRIN - Your knowledge has value

Der GRIN Verlag publiziert seit 1998 wissenschaftliche Arbeiten von Studenten, Hochschullehrern und anderen Akademikern als eBook und gedrucktes Buch. Die Verlagswebsite www.grin.com ist die ideale Plattform zur Veröffentlichung von Hausarbeiten, Abschlussarbeiten, wissenschaftlichen Aufsätzen, Dissertationen und Fachbüchern.

Visit us on the internet:

http://www.grin.com/

http://www.facebook.com/grincom

http://www.twitter.com/grin_com

COMMERCIALIZATION OF TEXTILE INDUSTRY UNDER BRITISH RULE: ASSESSING THE PLIGHT OF ARTISANS IN WESTERN AND EASTERN INDIA

Introduction:

Textile industry held a pre-dominant position in the economic history of India. The industrial revolution had an over-whelming impact on domestic industries leading to far-reaching repercussions in the economic sphere. B.R Tomlinson in his work, *Economy of Modern India, 1860-1970* [1] points out that at the beginning of the English rule the Indian handicraft and textile industries used to supply about a quarter of all manufactured goods produced in the world. The domestic industries contributed to the majority of chief export items of the European trade. With the start of the Industrial revolution in the west, India's status as the chief supplier of textiles to the world relegated to the background. India became the dumping ground of raw materials for the rising English Industries. At the same time the country was a potential market for the influx of British manufactures. There is a considerable quantitative data from south, Central and Eastern India hinting at the general decline in textile production. The English industrialization had a subversive effect on spinning and home spun commodities. The Lancashire produced fine quality yarn had somehow wrecked the possibilities of yarn spinning in India. Tirthankar Roy points out that cotton textile is the most important example of craft threatened by steam-power technology, or of pre-modern industry threatened by industrializing Britain [2].

Francis Crouzet claims that the process of industrialization in England was endogenous and it was occasioned by concatenation of circumstances. The industrial revolution opened a new age of promise. David Landes says that the massive technological progress preceded a change in the process of production in the economy. Landes mentions that the cotton manufacture was the most important in the kingdom in value of product, capital invested, and number of workers employed. The price of yarn took a downward course in England. Landes claims that the cheapest Hindu labour could not compete in either quality or quantity with Lancashire's mules and throstles. [3] This had further, accentuated the danger for the single overarching textile industry in India. Roy mentions that the threat initially came from Lancashire until pre-war decade and from Bombay in the inter-war period. [4] My paper operates at the interstices of two main lines of enquires, firstly, did the textile industry in India succumb due to the unequal nature of the contest? Secondly, how did the handlooms adapted to competition and how artisans responded to big changes in the market?

---

[1] B.R Tomlinson,' the economy of Modern India: 1860-1970', published by the Cambridge University Press, 1996.

[2] Tirthankar Roy,' Traditional Industry in the economy of Colonial India', published by the Cambridge University Press, 1999.

[3] David Landes, 'The unbound Prometheus ', published by the Cambridge University Press, 1969.

[4] Tirthankar Roy, 'Traditional Industry in the economy of Colonial India',1999

Commercialization and foreign trade

The British rule heralded a new epoch of commercialization and exposure to foreign trade. Subsequently, this had transformed Indian textiles in basic ways. Commercial hand-spinning of cotton became extinct due to competition from British rule and Indian machine spun-yarn. Roy mentions that the production of cotton cloth expanded by 30% between 1900 and 1939. Market shares were stable. New investments were made. New tools and processes like - flying shuttle, beam warping were appropriated on a large scale. In southern and western India, there was an endeavour to revamp textile mills along western lines which led to the growth of large urban textile towns. At the same time wage labour multiplied in place of family labour.[5]

The main deficit, emphasised by the *Indian Central Cotton Committee* in 1921 that while other countries, particularly America and England had powerful organizations to safeguard the interests concerning growing, marketing and manufacturing of cotton. India lacked organization and co-operation amongst the trade, their grower and the manufacturer. The Committee reports that while the production of long staple cotton was only 13% of total production in the quinquennium 1922-27, it increased to 37% in the quinquennium 1942-47 just before the partition of India.[6]

Speaking about the commercialization in handloom weaving, the picture was much more dynamic and compatible with the image of a violent and regressive exposure to foreign trade. In the inter-war period, surveys of the industry, produced in the course of the *Tariff Board Enquires* (during the period 1926-40 for textiles) and the *Fact Finding Committee report* produced mixed impressions. Until recently, de-industrialization history ignored 'diversification' or 'segmentation' within textile industry and talked about the experience of the weaver. But from about the middle of the 1980s, as Roy points out, scholars began to pay closer attention to the divisions within the industry. They postulated three broad hypotheses regarding the survival of the handloom weaving, which Professor Roy brought within the purview of consciousness. First, the existence of segmented markets for cloth, and the advantage of handloom over power loom which enabled some weavers to continue their work and prosper. Secondly, segmented markets imply that, quite apart from power loom competition, there was another force at work, changes in consumption. Thirdly, the surviving segments experienced organisational changes, and the impetus derived from various sources: long-distanced trade, competition among handloom weavers, and long circumstances such as migration created a large pool of hireable workers.[7]

Morris d. Morris underscores the condition of Bengal textile industry which dwindled into insignificance in the high noon of colonialism. He says that the machine made goods of Manchester had no match with the hand made goods of India. But the weavers were largely benefitted from the low price imported yarn. It is to be noted that the per-capita consumption of cloth augmented between 1800 and1847. Thus, the effective demand for handloom cloth was on rise. His thesis was challenged by Tapan Ray Chaudhuri, Bipan Chandra, and Toru Matsui in an article published in Indian Economic and Social History Review in 1968. They pointed out that the Indian weavers were

---

[5] Ibid

[6] Cotton grower's prosperity through improved varieties: published by Indian Central cotton committee, 1959, PG 1-5.

[7] Tirthankar Roy, 'Traditional industry in the economy of Colonial India', 1999

benefitted from low-price imported yarn. But Morris shunned two basic things: Firstly, the ruin of domestic spinners and the problems engendered by the declining prices of woven cloth. They showed in their paper that the living condition of Indian spinners and weavers was deplorable and they were not advantaged by the cost-reducing technological innovation founded in England.[8]

Let us examine the condition of cotton textile manufacturing centres in western and Central India. The commercial manufacture of cloth had long been associated with urban places in western India. At the beginning of Colonialism, many older centres receded as the indigenous textile industry was ebbing. Douglas E. Haynes claims by the late 19th century, with the revival of demand for handloom goods in the presidency cities and rural areas, artisanal production began to contribute to urban growth. Thousands of weavers began to drift to towns and small cities of Bombay Presidency, which was the business and commercial hub of India. They took up textile manufacturing as their full-time work, settled in their neighbourhood alongside fellow artisans, forged harmonious relationship and reframed identity centring their occupation. Mercantile actors, mostly from Gujarat and Maharashtra, dispersed into producing centres of western India, taking up the sale of yarn, the marketing of cloth and the control of production. The capitalism of small towns consolidated over the subsequent decades.[9] *Report of the Fact-finding committee (handloom and mills)* says in 1942, half of the Presidency's looms were located in its largest twenty-six centres; total production was even more concentrated in these places.[10]

The growth of weaving in towns located in Marathi-speaking districts of the Bombay is doubtless, remarkable. During the late 19th century, there was a proliferation of weaving centres concentrated in Sholapur, Ahmednagar, Malegaon, Yeola, and Bhiwandi. So, there was a substantial regional realignment of petty production within Western India. Douglas E. Haynes claims in Northern parts of the Presidency, particularly in Gujarat, the growth in artisanal centres came to a halt. The town of Dholka in Ahmednagar district, where cheap Khadi garments were produced in abundance until 1887, gradually faded off. Ahmadabad, itself reduced into insignificance as a handloom centre. Surat was the only exception in the gloomy picture, where various kinds of artisanal activities sustained because of over-seas demand. In Khandesh, where cloth manufacturing was phenomenal in the 18th century, production also stagnated under British rule. Dhulia, as Haynes says, remained a significant manufacturing centre. Artisanal production of cloth constituted a colossal portion of economy of weaving towns.[11] The 1942 *Report of the Fact-Finding Committee* estimated that weaver formed 75% of the population in Guledgud and 'nearly all' of the population in Ilkal in western India.[12] Many of these towns, as the Report suggests, crystallized into 'weaving places' or christened the 'mono-industrial' centres.

---

[8] Bipan Chandra and T. Raychaudhuri,' Re-interpretation of 19th century Indian Economic History', published by Indian Economic and Social History Review, 1968.

[9] Douglas E. Haynes, Small town capitalism in Western India: Artisans, merchants and the making of informal economy, 1870-1960, published by the Cambridge University Press, 2012, pg-56-57.

[10] Government of India: *Report of the Fact-Finding Committee (*Handloom and Mills) (Calcutta: Government of India press, 1942), pg-67.

[11] Douglas E. Haynes, Small town capitalism in Western India: Artisans, merchants and the making of informal economy, 1870-1960, published by the Cambridge University Press, 2012, pg-58.

[12] Report of the Fact-Finding Committee, Pg-66.

Speaking in a nut-shell, there is no consensus of opinions among scholars regarding the chequered career of textile industry which found an important mention in the de-industrialization history. Undoubtedly, the English Industrialization spawned an economic tumult in Asian Landmass, particularly in India, making the country subservient to English manufactures and debauching her handicraft industries. However, the artisans were in quest for segmentation or diversification of textile industries and accommodate new changes. This propelled them to prosper and continue their profession in the changing economic condition.

Notes

Secondary sources:

B.R Tomlinson,' the economy of Modern India: 1860-1970', published by the Cambridge University Press, 1996.

Tirthankar Roy,' Traditional Industry in the economy of Colonial India', published by the Cambridge University Press, 1999.

David Landes, 'The unbound Prometheus ', published by the Cambridge University Press, 1969.

Bipan Chandra and T. Raychaudhuri,' Re-interpretation of 19th century Indian Economic History', published by Indian Economic and Social History Review, 1968.

Douglas E. Haynes, Small town capitalism in Western India: Artisans, merchants and the making of informal economy, 1870-1960, published by the Cambridge University Press, 2012.

Primary sources:

Cotton grower's prosperity through improved varieties: published by Indian Central cotton committee, 1959.

Government of India: *Report of the Fact-Finding Committee (*Handloom and Mills) (Calcutta: Government of India press, 1942.